NATIVE HEART

NEKITA ROBERTS

ILLUSTRATED BY
JACLYN ROBERTS

All correspondence to the publisher

Nekita Roberts
Email: info@theaustralianpoet.com
www.theaustralianpoet.com

© Copyright Nekita Roberts

First Printed 2016

The right of Nekita Roberts to be identified as the author of this work
and Jaclyn Roberts to be identified as the illustrator of this work, has been
asserted by them in accordance with the Copyright, Designs and Patents act.

All rights reserved. No part of this publication may be reproduced,
stored in or introduced into a retrieval system, or transmitted, in any form,
or by any means (electronic, mechanical, photocopying, recording or otherwise)
without the prior written permission of the publisher. Any person who does any
unauthorised act in relation to this publication may be liable to criminal prosecution
and civil claims for damages.

This book is sold subject to the condition that it shall not, by way of trade
or otherwise, be lent, re-sold, hired out, or otherwise circulated without the
publisher's prior consent in any form of binding or cover other than that in
which it is published and without a similar condition including this condition
being imposed on the subsequent purchaser.

Written and arranged by Nekita Roberts

Illustrations by Jaclyn Roberts

ISBN 978-0-9953645-0-9

Category: Poetry: Author

FOR INDY & SKY

&

HARLAN

For Dr Alison Hadley

she was a smart little girl
the same age as me
from the western suburbs of sydney
switched on with an inquisitive mind
mathematics came to her easily
i was a kid from the ocean side
who loved to write
we were art and science
worlds apart and now i owe her mine
the little girl who saved my life

CONTENTS

PREFACE	9
Chapter 1 - ANIMAL	**13**
animal	15
house	16
lions	16
words	19
skin	20
kids	20
stars	23
dark horse	23
life	24
need	24
insect	27
nothing	27
writer	28
driftwood	28
mum	31
beautiful	31
river	32
fight	32
Chapter 2 - FIRESTORM	**35**
headlights	37
gone	37
sparks	38
neon	41
stage	42
drive	45
Nora	45
fly	46
glance	46
storm	49
torn	49
you	50
wake	53
stranger	53

Chapter 3 - LOST IN PARADISE   **55**

   peace   57
   sands   57
   deep blue sea   58
   sunshine   61
   earth   61
   hinterland   62
   little cove   65
   wild   66
   sacred land   66
   miles   69
   ocean   69
   still   70
   parts   70
   Noosa   73
   old tree   74
   inside   77
   giants   77
   element   78
   moonlight   78
   listen   81
   force of nature   81

Chapter 4 - BLUE MOON   **83**

   moon   85
   alone   85
   life   86
   lest we forget   86
   shipwrecked   89
   dream   89
   gold   90
   home   90
   thunder   93
   blues   93
   myth   94
   blanket   94
   George   97
   the ticket   98
   galaxy   101
   maths   102
   cub   105

canopy	105
seeds	106
rain	106
shooting star	109
lost	109

Chapter 5 - CRAZY LITTLE WORLD — **111**

dance	113
holiday	113
chaos	114
princess	114
up late	117
missing	117
castle	118
reckless	121
sunday	121
gosling	122
hometown	125
stash	125
easy	126
barry	129
trouble	129
colours	130
love	130

Chapter 6 - THE ROMANTIC — **133**

art	135
blood red	135
forever young	136
up here	139
chrome	139
light	140
high	140
rocks	143
shack	143
universe	144
planet	144
Jessie	147

Chapter 7 - STORYTELLER — **149**

songwriter	151

masterpiece	152
blind	155
falling	156
bitter	159
other side	160
grounded	160
fields	163
winter	164
island	164
faraway	167
trees	167
king of the track	168

Chapter 8 - WELCOME TO THE JUNGLE — 171

mind	173
evolution	173
waves	174
fence me in	174
death wish	177
poetry	177
still	178
tomahawk	178
bare	181
heavy	181
bleed	182
fear	182
ego	185
broken	185
survive	186
façade	186
caught	189
peace	189
night	190
puppy love	190
machine	193
lover	193
mine	194
green	194
garden	197
muse	197
the poet	198

PREFACE

I still write my words into the sand like I did back then.....

His eyes were green like the hilltops we would run to. Up there, the grass was lush and springy under our feet. When the rain had been, the rolling hills were like sheets of velvet or a magic carpet. We would just fly up to our place. Sometimes up there in our tree house they would be blue, his eyes I mean, brilliant blue with yellow stars around the pupils. I could look away and then back and they would be green again. When I said so he would smile and roll his eyes a little bit, "A chameleon you say?" flicking his tongue to make me laugh. He thought I had a great imagination, "the best in the whole wide world." But when the seas were rough and the winds were angry, he would stare out past the whipping palm prongs and out beyond the ocean. Now his eyes were deep and dark, like the unsettled waters below. It always seemed like he was looking at something in particular, like a pirate ship or someone lost at sea, but I could never see anything. When the skies were wild, I always felt safe. What's more, we had built this tree house like a fortress. It was by far our strongest one. We'd collected all of the wood and ropes from an old boat that had shattered on the rocks one night. And his knots were better than any scouts.

From here I could watch the trees dance. With every sweeping, howling gust of wind they would each come to life. Every tree had a rhythm of its own. Some danced in slow motion to the peaceful storm. The long grass on the dunes thrashed around like crazy. Two tall pines swayed together like twins, looking as though they might snap clean in half. When he finally turns away from the crashing waves, he is tired and I know he'll need to rest before the afternoon's work. He makes some notes in the tree house logbook and takes a few bites of his peach before falling asleep to the sound of raindrops on the canopy above. The journal was important for our work on the island I write...

1. Collect palm prongs to fix roof thatching.
2. Gather berries and fruit for the box.
3. Check on the animals after the storm.

I cross out the last point. He has already mentioned it.
He writes...

1. A wild storm blew in today. Check on the island's animals.
2. Replace frayed rope on trap door.
3. Check the bamboo water pipes for leaves.
4. Her eyes are a stormy grey, blue colour with a light blue star around the pupil and a dark blue ring around the edge.

The wind is still singing as I smile and drift off to sleep beside him knowing that I'll be up at first light like I always am, to drag my driftwood words into the sand...

Chapter 1

ANIMAL

animal

if you feel misunderstood
indecipherable
incomprehensible
if you feel like you're
unfathomable
remember you're just an animal

house

stand in
your house
with your
heart of gold
guard your
totem animal
and your
beautiful people
be humble
and respect
your elders
bow down
only to
mother nature

lions

if they're waiting on me
to tell someone else who to be
they may as well
throw me to the lions

words

their words are made of cold hard steel
bolted together like super structures
arching over lonely cities
the lost and weary underneath
fading away like rusty pylons
our words are built with ropes and planks
and things we find along the way
they're bound together against the odds
stretched across dividing ranges
they're the bridges that we string together
our words are for the hearts and minds

skin

look him
straight in the eye
really look in
he can only fit
so much ink
on his skin

kids

we were kids dark and light
played together in the red dirt
and i still hold you up so high
the secret for this land you hold it
the sorrow in your heart i'd take it

but i cannot wear the shame
of a time before I walked this earth
cannot hang my head in their name
i can only take you for who you are
and you can only take me the same

stars

some people insist
they have nothing in common
but we're all here
in the same speck of time
on the same little planet
under the same lonely stars
that's got to be something

dark horse

always the black sheep
you were the lone wolf
i've got a feeling
you're the dark horse

life

each day she reads
another page
precious chapters
paper thin
this fresh ink
she breaths it in
a life written
in non-fiction

need

tell me what you want
all your dreams
silk dresses
shiny cars
but don't tell me what you need
not unless you speak of
water shelter food
or love

insect

beware the
fierce competitor
claiming victory
in the contest
you never even entered
on your every move
like an ambush predator
they'll have you
in their focus
waiting for the kill
like a praying mantis

nothing

he knew everything
about everything
and nothing
it seemed
about anything

writer

he was a writer for sure
ink stained fingertips
fine line paper cuts
and those
someplace else eyes
running deep
beneath a heavy brow

driftwood

the lonely and discarded
we can't know
from what they've come
we don't know
just where they've been
like washed up bits of driftwood
thrown out from the high seas

mum

dark
haired
long
legged
cool
calm
gentle
strong
musical
unusual
classic
beauty
to behold

beautiful

you can grow old
but I can't see it
just as beautiful
as you ever were

river

ornithorhynchus anatinus
thinking back to how they tried to sink us
drown this valley undulating
flood this fertile land just take it
murder for the dam they're making
fools in suits can't understand
why he's making plans for rope's end
his life work, his dignity, his home
all gone
so ornithorynchus
beak like a duck tail like a beaver
little platypus so strange and shy
don't like the spotlight
and peculiar lung fish deep in the mary
just thinking about how we won this fight

fight

are you going to
fight for it
or not?

Chapter 2

FIRESTORM

headlights

he was a fast car
she was a sunday drive
on their own roads
always meant to collide
and it was a wreck
yet somehow sweet sublime
thinking back
to a moment in time
her radio blasting
driving into the night
windows down
hair flying wild
just shadows of him now
in her headlights

gone

it was love at
first sight
gone in the flash
of a traffic light

sparks

wild child
it's true
i could've died
when you smiled
wildflowers
we always ran
like crazy
through the
rain showers
wildfire
you and i sent sparks
up to the sky
and even higher

neon

i swim
in and out
of constellations
into the deep
past electric strangers
an underwater rave
of neon wonder
fang tooth monsters
i need a surface
to gasp for life
to roll in sheets of plankton
in an ocean beneath a sky

stage

she was a theatre
he was her stage
it was a dramatic script
she was on every page
walking the boards
in her five inch heels
a stellar performance
of a jealous rage
and it was only ever really
a one act play
so madly in love
with her mirror of lights
roll out the red carpet
she's on the
big screen tonight
and he kicks himself
every chance he gets
he could have
shared that milkshake
with the girl next door
and just rode off
into the sunset

drive

he tossed her the key
to his idling heart
and said
drive it like you stole it

Nora

she always hated her name
shy - and the glaring spotlight
men - they always came first
sister - best friend lost in childbirth
blue eyes - running deep as the river
swear - she could roll with the best
heels - always a lady
suspicious - the world's greatest cynic
laugh - till you could hardly breath
secrets - gates locked till the end
family - all that she'd need

fly

we burn it to the night sky
just to watch the embers fly
while they stare into the flames
hand in hand we run away
find a place we're free to soar
where the deep blue surging ocean roars
watch the sunrise in each other's eyes
knowing
this is paradise

glance

don't look my way
if it's not real emotion
i am not your fleeting glance
i am devotion
i am not your breaking waves
i am the ocean

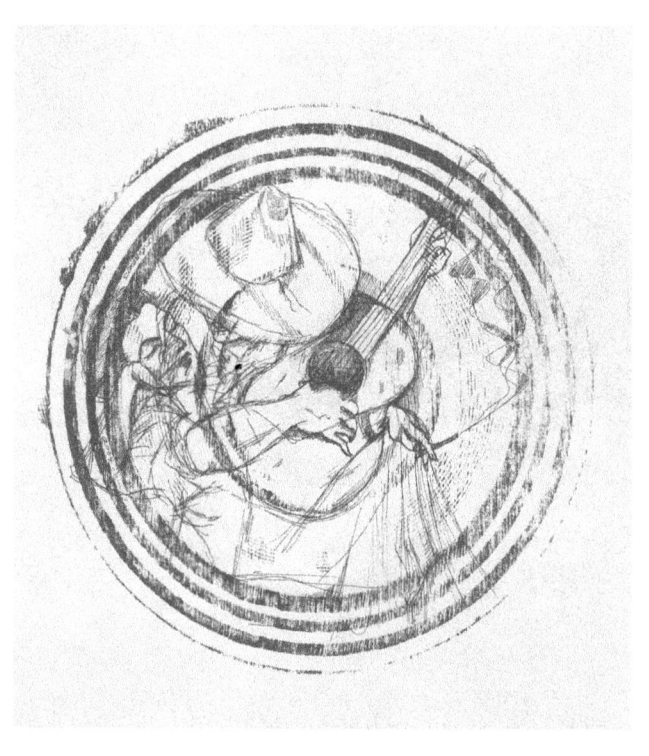

storm

the bureau says
scattered showers
with the possibility
of a late afternoon storm
still i wait here
under darkened skies
for the kind of thunder
that stops the heart
for torrential rain
gale force winds
give me something
that tears the roof off

torn

woven into him
a recurring dream
forgotten
at the bottom of
the mending pile
ripped and torn
where they left him
waiting for
a steady hand
to thread him

you

we were kids
skimming stones
building fortresses
with sticks
lighting fires by the creek
to burn them to the ground
salt water in our cuts
got the same kinda scars
we ran to ocean caves
when the sky fell down
and it's crazy how you say
it was always me
when we were miles apart
funny how we were looking
at the same stars
our rivers reaching
to the same sea
and it was only ever you

wake

his final note
it resonates
and they all say
what a shame
but she strikes a match
and lights a flame
sending him off
into the clear night
singing his song
to the moonlight
and on this ride
she is all in
for the love
for the life
for the music

stranger

they both
looked back
like they knew
but what could they do?
they were
dark strangers
passing on a misty night

Chapter 3

LOST IN PARADISE

peace

come in peace
take only what
you need

sands

these sands
belong to no
hourglass
as i belong
to no city
by these
freedom tides
we roll
for we belong
to the sea

deep blue sea

if i'm so hard to find
stop looking in the wrong place
back then you would count
and i would hide
with the widest smile
you'd yell, found ya!
now you look high and low
yet we're still those kids
sky blue horizons, oceans before us
bare feet to the earth, kissing the land
path to our hearts, that old beach track
driftwood words, dragged in the sand
but i can't see you now under these waves
open your stormy eyes and find your way here
i wanna swim with you in the deep blue sea

sunshine

i knew her eyes shot lightning
and her heart made thunder
yet with her single tear
still I was struck by wonder
it was only a butterfly
and some wilted flowers
in the sunshine

earth

such beauty
to go back
to the earth
and become
the air that
we all breath

hinterland

sunrise through the haze
we go west to a little town
to lose ourselves in time
meander in a market maze
with flavours so exotic
roasted coffee aromatic
takes me to another place
the mountain of a king
to look for antique things
past the sunlit chrome
of a chariot strung with
lengths of white silk ribbon
and then this grand hotel
beyond a century old
her piano in the corner
not yet sung its last song
and on the side of the roads
all the fruit of the gods
abundant and organic
and in this amphitheatre
across the still blue water
by her lake house dream
he gives away his daughter
with everything to live for
in these gardens to die for
and i know that there is still
gold here in these hills
as we drive towards the
endless sands stretched out
before this wonderland

little cove

you walked from devil's kitchen
through hell's gates
past the wildest seas
to get to me
where the deep blue ocean
meets the lush green land
a natural paradise
laced in sand
a place where i
can close my eyes
to the ancient rhythms
of another time
here with you
i don't need a thing
it feels like little cove
in the spring
or tea tree bay
on a perfect day
like warm granite rocks
beneath my feet
like the whole wide world
doesn't matter to me
like i'd leave it all behind
in a heartbeat

wild

she knew
his heart
because
she came
from the wild

sacred land

don't forget
where we stand
here on sacred land
cause you're
shredding her up
like your
pieces of paper
prancing around
like we were born
in skyscrapers

miles

give me miles and miles of nothing
insects smashed in my grill
red dust clouds in my rearview
wedge tail eagles on roadkill
cup of teas on the tailgate
music, philosophies
laughter, epiphanies
and the time of my life
with my best mate

ocean

respect her
and she'll be
the best friend
you ever had

still

like a solo bird
looking for its mate
flew too high
too low
too bent
too straight
remember when they said
if you get lost
in the carnival
to just stand still
In the one place

parts

had a heart
so savaged
war ravaged
sent back from
a hopeless place
ruin and carnage
treading lightly
over land mines
left to pick up
all the parts
lost between
the ending
and the start

Noosa

morning dew
on the gum leaves
and he can't really see
through the windscreen
kicking it over and
she starts first time
warming her up
before the break of light
single fins on the roof racks
dust and her in the rear view
and this little town feels like
the jewel in the crown
and that little dirt road
is all dressed up now
all her shifting sands
her changing tides
but she stays the same
her long clean lines
her perfect curves
forever blue
and when she stands tall
they stand in awe
she's a festival
a point break dream
a timeless beauty queen

old tree

old tree it seems to me your time is up
you stand tall but all i see
are broken branches bleeding sap leaves curled
generations have breathed you in
children have climbed
lovers have laid
here in the light of your dappled sun
initials and hearts
carved with pocket knives
your trunk wears the scars
of our beautiful lives
but they're coming most days now
in their suits and ties to sell us the lies
i would stop all this madness if only i could
but there are power lines that need your place in the sky
and a steel pole that needs to stand where you stood
I could not stop that tear that escaped from my eye
they'll call me a tree hugger so they can all sleep at night
we could see mountains up there in your treetop
and i've got a little piece of you in my wooden slingshot
goodbye old tree

inside

under waterfalls
she swims with you
floats in the crystal creek
lays here in the sunshine
dreaming wild and free
she takes you to her garden
and talks to you at night
falling asleep together
beneath the soft moonlight
she feels you deep
inside her heart
in her flesh and blood
with eyes still yet to meet
you're both already in love

giants

killing ocean giants
to call it science
and i've never
seen a human
look so small

element

on the whitest sand
by the deepest ocean
we light the highest flames
under the clearest skies
earth water air and fire

moonlight

all the colours of the ocean in the setting sun
turquoise waves lit with amber light
jumping off the rocks into the deepest blue
on the east coast as day becomes night

she's down on the beach, the horizon beyond
salt in her hair and fire in her eyes
he's on his last wave and she's home right here
she sees him now paddling in with the boys

they stay until the darkness sets in
and the last butterflies play in the dunes
she knows everything's right, just as it should be
as they skate home under the moon

listen

you speak so loud
running your race
at the speed of sound
yet you can't hear
the far off thunder
the ocean at night
the earth's vibrations
for the noise in your head
and you're telling them
to turn it down
death metal
going straight to hell
and while you're cursing
every decibel
i think
you're just not listening

force of nature

underestimate her
and you'll find out
what she's made of

Chapter 4

BLUE MOON

moon

when your ship goes down
and your sky falls in
look for a shard of light
and your broken mast
build a little raft
and sail it to the moon

alone

solitude
just me
the moon
the stars
my mind
my heart

life

life, it picked us one by one
always knew my time would come
just had too much to lose I guess
new baby girl up on my chest
poison surging through my veins
golden locks, stripped away
cut me. I cried like a child
radiate me. I still smiled
with love and science at my side
fighting death in strong alliance
i came out standing in the sun
hair flying wild, new life begun

lest we forget

when I close my eyes
i see a part of life
in every shade of blue
the world you sacrificed

shipwrecked

you got me
shipwrecked
on your shore
stranded here
for evermore
not even the wind
can take me home
not even time
can bring you back

dream

if you're dying
inside
dream yourself
to life

gold

there's a thrill
a type of rush in panning for gold
and my heart's already plated
with what you seek
but i'll let the cool water wash over me
as I float downstream in the creek
while you fossick for flakes of what we used to be
and i know that you don't see me

home

he wasn't given
half a chance
just a little kid
without a home
now they're rolling
in the aisles for him
while he stands
up there
and takes the piss
and it makes him think
he might just be
strong enough
to live through this

thunder

a quiet thunder in his heart
always rumbled in the distance
with words only dogs could here
mumbled and whispered
an awkward beauty
with dark smiling eyes
and man's best friend
loyal at his side
when they said he was gone
i thought it awfully strange
that with all that he had
there was nothing he could change
that with all of the treasure
there was nothing he could find
here on this beautiful earth
to make it worthwhile

blues

don't look for me
in the brightest hues
find me in faded
shades of indigo
in dusted sunlight
on my windowsill
singing the sweetest
blues

myth

broken and forlorn
she whistles for her unicorn
and as the final pieces plummet
rides the lightning to the summit
he's up there on his pegasus
rocks falling from his precipice
she smiles at him and draws her bow
through his heart her straightest arrow
to his lips her final kiss
nothing more than a beautiful myth

blanket

impossible skies
over sacred land
under this blanket
i will tuck you in

George

he put his roots down
in this fertile soil
for them to come
and rip it all away
to rape this earth for
coal seam gas
to cut a deal for
sleepless nights
until the water didn't
flow the same
until his mighty heart
was finally broken
they can wash their hands
but they're stained in red
for what they've really taken
it's their time now
to toss and turn
for these fallen fences
and barbed wire endings

the ticket

i've got this ticket
tattered in my pocket
taped back together
had it since forever
there's no fine print
it's unconditional
redeemable
i can spend it how i want to
on the ocean
on the sky
in his eyes
on the kid who jumps the train
i'm not a smart ass about it
but i never have to doubt it
won't ever tear it up again
and if you never got one
if you got left behind
don't worry
i can lend you mine

galaxy

the barmaid's calling last drinks
he's still here on his own stool
a fading galaxy of memories
back when he was captain cool
with his rocket ship of pretty girls
venus mercury jupiter mars
and he had the entire universe
but he missed the shooting star

maths

to sum it up
the subtraction
of affection
and addition
of addiction
equates to
a fraction
of the passion
and multiplication
of frustration
and I'm no
mathematician
but it's not
long division

cub

you lost your lion
to the merciless wild
always his sidekick
back here in your element
with your lioness and brother
crouched before this predator
his little beauty
a fearless warrior
with a heart as big as his
still right there beside him

canopy

i was lost in the woods
with these tiny shards
of splintered light
piercing through
the canopy
and straight into
my beating heart

seeds

he threw his last seeds
at the hopeless dust
then sat in his spot
on the old verandah
day after day
with the forgotten
scent of her
and the rain
that never came

rain

when the earth
is cracking
beneath your feet
just sit back
and wait for the rain

shooting star

what good is the
entire universe
if you miss
the shooting star?

lost

they lost each other
never to be seen
like a pair of socks
in the washing machine

Chapter 5

CRAZY LITTLE WORLD

dance

she's back in the kitchen once again
steam dancing off the sink
kettle on, tunes up loud
morning sunlight on her skin
in her old t-shirt she pirouettes
ties the hair back off her face
body arches to the bench
leg kicks high in her skirt of lace
and they say she chose the menial life
destined to be someone's stepford wife
but she knows love just as well as pain
and has music running through her veins
so i'd have to say that's not the case
dropping it now like she's the baddest in the place

holiday

what a shame to
spend a whole life
and never realise
this is the holiday

chaos

don't come into
my crazy little world
and mess up
my sweet chaos

princess

they'll try to
put you in a box
like you can't be
anything you want to be
little princess on a flying fox

up late

i love those late night conversations
firing our words off in a barrage
yelling at each other
over the top of a blaring boom box
in the garage

missing

he was
broken down
battery flat
twisted wires
electrics gone
no connection
not firing
no spark
missing
lost keys
tank dry
out of gas
steering shot
cracked head
over the limit
written off
out of love

castle

she said
if you can
climb the mountain
and slay the dragon
and build me the castle
and drape me in silk
i'll wait for you there
with flowers in my hair
he said
forgive me
princess
you sound like
hard work

reckless

you say i'm
clumsy
reckless
too nice
gutless
messy
can't cook
too soft
a real sook
man you got
some issues

sunday

they come to my door
on a sunday
preaching at me
over barking dogs
and rampaging children
their eyeballs look weird
and I can't even hear them

gosling

she had fresh cut grass
homemade lemonade
yet adventure
was all that she craved
the eternal optimist
still looking for loch ness
big foot and yetis
elflings and erlkings
still waiting
on ryan gosling

hometown

we couldn't keep
this place a secret
and i know it was
never really ours
but when i see them
only look up
to look down
i think of us all
just mucking around
i can't help but smile
we owned this town

stash

down the back yard
under the big tree
in a rusty old tin
dug in dirt and ash
is where I keep my
secret poetry stash

easy

it won't be easy
even dangerous
near impossible they say
laced with affliction
tribulation
save yourself the pain
they sell me easy street
like some estate agent
desperate for the sale
the walk in the park
the secret shortcut
the seamless painless plan
just watch out it's not all there
waiting for you at the end
i'll take the long way home
through the
wrong neighbourhood
i'd rather pay my dues
maybe you don't understand
but not everyone's
looking for easy

barry

havin' a barry
and he hits the turps
gets in a bingle
with a bogan
at the back of bourke
now he's hammered
spewin' that he's
outta rollies
gonna run the gauntlet
he'd kill for a tallie
the cop's here now
says blow in the bag
don't come the raw prawn mate
you know you've got buckley's

trouble

he and i
we're cut from
the same cloth
just can't seem
to stay out
of trouble

colours

he said
come on
i found
this place
where they
hang colours
in the trees
where you
can be
whatever
you wanna be

love

If you
have
love
in
spades
give
some
away

Chapter 6

THE ROMANTIC

art

she took a little
piece of sandpaper
to his wooden heart
and buffed it into
a work of art

blood red

this evening dear
i shall write you a letter
at my old oak desk
on my finest paper
in a beautiful script
with the blackest ink
sealed with a kiss
and blood red wax
i shall sign my name
forever yours

forever young

stepping out of the ocean
in the autumn breeze
timber speed boat on the water
like some james bond scene
got that bo derek style
in her crochet bikini
her bicycle parked up
beside that lamborghini
rocking retro shades
washing off her feet
slipping into her high top
blue denim jeans
riding out through the woods
where she first saw him
past the old gondola
where her beating heart sings
over the little bridge
to the farmer's market
children jumping in the river
fresh flowers in her basket
then she's home to him
he's got the morning news
still looking at her
like she's his only muse
and in her hands
she sees a life well spent
couldn't really tell you
where the years went
but here in this place
on this earth in his arms
she would be forever young

up here

up here with you
there are no words

chrome

remember that night
we were dressed so fine
you picked me up
in your white wall tyres
you looked me over with
those sparkling eyes
and we went riding
to the otherside
i'm still beside you
on that old bench seat
home here
with your arm around me
we sure put some miles on that clock
you and i
driving in the clear moonlight
chrome still shining bright

light

through my lens
you're right in focus
bathed in the refracting light
saturated in colours blue
reflecting from my eyes
set my shutter speed and aperture
to capture you forever
like in my heart, like i said
until the end of never

high

she comes in on a sugar high
flour dusted on her cheeks
vanilla scent on milky skin
maple syrup on her lips
eggshell broken on the bench
jumping in his sunlit sheets.
says morning sweetie.
Pancakes!

rocks

fishing off the rocks with you
until we're silhouettes
got my hook on tight
my rig just right
lines in the water
we're getting bites
and you're looking at me
like I'm not gonna be
the one that got away

shack

all he ever wanted
was a little wife
a baby on her hip
the ocean at his feet
and shack life

universe

she hails from old dundowran
where the tides stretch way out far
her dreams on the horizon
a young girl and her guitar

a love so great was waiting
the boy across the bay
an adventure like no other
the life she knows today

when she looks up to the sky at night
across the moon she roams
four stars shine bright together
the whole universe in her home

planet

on this earth
water we drink
air we breath
fires we light
we can't be the
only planet alive

Jessie

when she first lost her soldier she shed her tears
then she picked herself up and packed her suitcase
with just a few things and something nice to marry him in.
she caught the northbound train
to find him there with his best of mates
howling at the moon beneath the street lamp.
across wars and decades
they made a life so rich and full.
when she lost him again, her handsome soldier
she brushed herself off like the bravest of troopers.
she played her harmonica up on that stage.
it was pure gold the way she entertained.
and she was 98 when she dreamed herself away
and found him again on that sunny day.

Chapter 7

STORYTELLER

songwriter

you walk the long way home
fumbling keys at the door
no one's here now in the room
in this perfect solitude
only her in the corner
with her maple curves
glowing warm beneath the street light
in your embrace, the perfect fit
fingers slide along steel strings
you strum a chord, a minor e
so sad and yet so sweet
you whisper words and sing them low
it's beauty and magic
this little song
writing itself in your hands
then you scribble it down
on a torn piece of paper
just so it won't all be lost in time
beautiful, magical
songwriter of mine

masterpiece

it was a lighthearted girl
who stole his heavy heart away
he was the dark in the night
she was the light in the day
she was the tint on the palette
while he was the shade
bound together
by the colours they'd made
her pastels all over
his favourite black shirt
he'd painted her heart red
and torn her white skirt
it was no oil painting
the critics agreed
rather an obscure, abstract
contemporary
a post expressionist
surreal in its realism
figurative
futurist
epic
masterpiece

blind

she sits there in the library
labrador at her side, braids in her hair
slender fingers running gently
along clean, white paper
exploring embossed textures
every braille bump, every blank space
her intensity builds, as though consumed
dangerous and desperate
devouring mountains and valleys now
i think I can see her
standing on the headland
in her billowing dress
wild hair lashing at her face
she's grabbing at pieces of a rainbow
stuffing them madly into her pockets
like stolen jewels
i see her irises, open shutters
light spilling into her dilated pupils
like a lover climbing through
her window at night
lost in a world all of her own
like the only passenger
on the last rocket to the moon
she shuts her open book
buttons her faded yellow cardigan
to walk home in the dark
every bird clear as a whistle
the midday sun warm on her face

falling

you were playing king
when you fell from the treetops.
i bet it felt like slow motion
it was shutter speed
your arched back
cracking over
splintered rungs
foliage stripped bare
rope burn hands
body broken
impaled
no time to exhale
you did good!
ringbarked your beautiful life
lost forever, your golden crown
took out a nest full of baby birds
on your way down

bitter

she was a bitter woman
who had managed to suck
every last bit of romance and joy
out of her life
everything about me bothered her
the way I smelt the flowers
and found shapes in the clouds
the way I didn't care for shoes
or her mind numbing practicality
when I smiled or laughed
or shrugged my shoulders
and walked in the rain
she was livid
surely she could see
that with me
she would only ever be fighting
a losing battle

other side

we were born in waves
always there
breaking on our shoulders
but we could see the other kind
on a distant shore
bet we could swim with sharks
make it there and back
live how we always dreamed
oh well friend
guess it all went wrong
somewhere along the line
we were just young and stupid
now they're eating us alive

grounded

stay grounded
in this
boundless world

fields

moving through the fields
like a queen past the shirtless gods
her never ending legs
turning heads in the heat wave
glistening, golden beads
rolling clean down their spines
with her hyper colour eyes
cast beyond to open skies
basket on her swaying hips
ripened fruit brought to her lips
before the wealthy farmer's son
she kneels now, bowing down
dirty nails, summer dress
cotton blouse come undone
another day of yearning
in her bittersweet eternity
strawberry picking
underneath the blazing Australian sun

winter

i know that you'll be
cool
like the summer rain
strong
like the autumn breeze
beautiful
like the blooms in spring
enchanting
like the winter

island

the old squatter
and the wild goats
watch over your shores
while the tourists
sit hunched
in glass bottom boats
and the suits squawk on
about culling wild goats
and building casinos
and eco resorts
and you lay here
in the coral sea
basking in the sun
like an island queen

faraway

he escaped
from the coldest winter
a hibernation
that almost stopped his heart
it was a fair haired girl
with a pack of wolves
who came everyday
and chipped away
i heard she took his hand
before the frost bite could
they say she led him off
to some faraway place
where he died
in a field of sunshine

trees

we climb these trees to see
dreams like these

king of the track

i'd always wait out the front of your house
faded blue jeans, bubble gum in my mouth
wonder woman t-shirt, on my malvern star
spokey dokes, streamers on my handle bars

grease on your face from fixing your chain
and smiling because i was here again
you'd say, race ya, come on. you ride like a girl
i was your favourite person in the whole wide word

your dad was evel knievel but was never around
stunt pegs in the mail box and you were ruling the town
down at the track you'd have to fight for your bike
fight for your go and for the girl that you liked

i remember all of those times and all of my stacks
you'd lock it up sideways and mono straight back
dink me to the tap, wash the blood from my knees
then say that it would always be me

and you made that jump with the sun in your eyes
i knew you would. it was no surprise
i can still see you wiping the sweat from your brow
and i don't even know where you are now

but to me
you'll forever be
the king of the track

Chapter 8

WELCOME TO THE JUNGLE

mind

it was a brave and foolish voyager
who set out on the ocean wild
a navigator of the great unknown
lost at sea in her treacherous mind
the next one was a watchmaker
a master craftsman in his own right
tried to fit her together like clockwork
her intricate mind left him far behind
the last one was a carpenter's son
he knew he'd need an entire lifetime
he was the one that she made hers
the one who blew her mind

evolution

there's change in the air
a shift in the ocean bed
transformation
beneath the leaves
it's evolution baby

waves

she comes to him in waves
barreling in then closing out
he's caught inside her shore break
heavy dumping drowning doubt
she's messed up and wild tonight
then clean and offshore
come morning light
but he'll hold on tight
for the ride of his life
she's a left and then a right

fence me in

i don't mind
if you fence me in
for a little while
before I take
this place apart
before I run
like the wind

death wish

i led you to the well
but could not make you drink
dropped in
my gleaming gold
if only to watch it sink
locked in
our vampire eyes
so piercing
devilish
while you threw in your last coin
on a whim and a death wish

poetry

i may never be that brilliant
just not broken enough
far too resilient
not to get back up
exemplary vocabulary
no desire for fancy words
i can tell you a story
sing to you in brilliant blue
maybe fly you to the moon
i'll take you to the heart of me
it's just a bit of poetry

still

like a solo bird
looking for its mate
flew too high
too low
too bent
too straight
remember when they said
if you get lost
in the carnival
to just stand still
In the one place

tomahawk

set down your trusty tomahawk
you grew this giant beanstalk
from one seed in the barren dirt
under ruthless skies you built this forte
vines twisting through the darkest cloud
to get to where you are right now
found out what it would really take
to learn from your mistakes
we can only tell it how it is
teach our kids to dream like this

bare

would it matter if the wind
messed up your hair?
if your feet got dirty
if your heart was laid bare?
would it be so bad
if the rain touched your skin?
would it kill you to let somebody in?

heavy

it'll get heavy
up against the elements
this surging ocean
building walls to break you with
or make you with
this falling sky forcing you
to run for cover or hold it up
but you're made of the same stuff
take on this mother
like a force of nature

bleed

he liked his eggs
over easy
his steak blue
and his poetry
still bleeding

fear

everyone's hating on fear right now
crushing him, kicking him out the door
his voice will kill you if you let it
but give the guy a bit of credit
he's the reason that you're screaming
on the roller coaster
and the guy who told you not to
stick the knife into the toaster

ego

egomaniacs.
i think
they think
i think
they're
awesome
really
i just think
they are
fools

broken

like a fine piece of china
in the washing machine
he smashed her heart
to smithereens

survive

this place will show you
what it takes to survive
how to find what you need
to build a fire inside
how to save yourself when
it throws you up against
the life and death of it

facade

of this great man
she was the pioneer
an adventurer
of the last frontier
it was the war inside
she came to find
lost is the way
of the troubled mind
worn is the path
of the reckless heart
a beckoning oasis
but a mirage
shattered is the facade

caught

lost his place
in the line up
now he's
caught inside
held under
for what
seems
a lifetime
lost his board
now he's out there
on his own trip
swept into
another rip
and still swimming
against it

peace

world peace
feels like
a pipe dream

night

they were children
of the night
skipping over
railway tracks
tripping in the
spooky shadows
making tricky tunes
playing their music
to the twinkly stars
howling at the sparkly moon

puppy love

they'll wanna tell you
this is puppy love
like what you have
can never be enough
they're gonna say
you threw it all away
on this little mongrel
who could not be tamed

She felt like an ornament, like a trophy or a piece of decoration. She belonged on someone's shelf

machine

always so stealth
on your covert operation
secrets of the heart
under strict surveillance
your powers of perception
dead on every time
a finely tuned machine
immune to my rhyme
over and over
they line up for the thrill
if only they knew
that you shoot to kill

lover

he was your classic hater
i mean
the guy walked in
like darth vader
in his black t-shirt
and his faded jeans
with his cigarette
and his jaded dreams
one look in his eyes
and he's blown his cover
this one's an
underground lover

mine

she said
hey kid
listen here
in this life
there's no rewind
i wish I'd known
all this time
i didn't have to
walk the line
that love was blind
and here to find
romance was
a state of mind
i didn't have to
walk behind
that all this time
the sky was mine

green

the grass is no greener
on the other side
it's all just
show ponies and
filtered light

garden

he was burnt into her
like the midday sun
under her skin
like a tattoo gun
she didn't mind the heat
as long as she could have
aloe vera in her garden
and the ocean at her feet

muse

she is
the artist
and the muse
the mother
and the child
the beauty
and the beast
if you let her
off the leash

the poet

poetry is a universe
she keeps in her locket
a reminder of the fight
he fought with that pen
of the metal strikes
that stole the night
of the love loaded
lead pencil war in his head
a torn and tattered page
that he carried to the end

www.ingramcontent.com/pod-product-compliance
Lightning Source LLC
Chambersburg PA
CBHW071849090426
42811CB00004B/535